My Father's Keeper:

Dealing With The Residue of An Absent Father

By

Vic Coleman

My Father's Keeper:
Dealing with the Residue of an Absent Father
By Vic Coleman

Published by:
Victor Coleman
7544 FM 1960 Road East #1015
Humble, TX 77346

ISBN-13: 978-0-578-51608-0

ESV: Study Bible : English Standard Version. Wheaton, Ill: Crossway Bibles, 2007. Print.

Scripture quotations taken from the New American Standard Bible® (NASB),
Copyright © 1960, 1962, 1963, 1968, 1971, 1972, 1973,
1975, 1977, 1995 by The Lockman Foundation
Used by permission. www.Lockman.org

Scripture quotations taken from the Amplified® Bible (AMPC),
Copyright © 1954, 1958, 1962, 1964, 1965, 1987 by The Lockman Foundation
Used by permission. www.Lockman.org

Contact Information:
Vic Coleman ✦ 7544 FM 1960 East #1015 ✦ Humble, TX ✦ 77346
VicColeman@yahoo.com ✦ VicColeman.com

Table of Contents

Introduction

Fatherlessness has reached epidemic levels in the United States. Children without fathers are more likely to perform poorly in school, to be members of gangs, to be incarcerated and to suffer a long list of other adverse effects. Unfortunately, the adverse effects don't stop at childhood; they carry on into adulthood. Men who grew up without fathers typically have difficulty processing the emotional scars created during their childhood. As a result, many of the wounds of fatherlessness carry on to the next generation.

The purpose of this book is to help men Biblically address the ill effects of fatherlessness, and the residue that's left long after they enter adulthood. This is done through the story of the relationship between my father and me. My father was absent much of my life, even before my parents divorced. Little did I know that one day I would become my father's caretaker. In his later years, my father was diagnosed with Alzheimer/dementia. He lived with my wife and me for ten months. Eventually I had to move him into an assisted living facility to provide him with the care he required. And most recently, he succumbed to a heart condition and passed away two days before Christmas. All during this time I provided the time, attention and financial support he required.

There are many ironies in this situation. One of them was that as I became my father's keeper – providing time, attention and financial support to a man who hardly devoted any attention to me since the time I stopped wearing diapers. My desire is to share some of my experiences and to help other men navigate the feelings and effects of being fatherless – and most importantly, to show how only through a growing, *devoted* personal relationship with Jesus Christ we overcome the negative residue of fatherlessness.

At the end of each chapter, there is a one-page personal Bible study section to address some of the topics covered in the chapter. I will warn you now, some of the questions and scriptures may be probing and "hit home", addressing some feelings you may have buried years ago. But that's okay. God's word is designed to penetrate the heart. It is in the heart where the Holy Spirit begins His healing process.

The Foundation

In order for you to get a more complete picture of the relationship between my dad and me, I need to provide a little background. It all starts with his childhood which is a little sketchy. But based on what I've been able to piece together from a few records and conversations with him, this is how it all started.

My dad was born in 1931. He was the middle child of five boys and one girl. His mother was Rebecca Shearer. She was married to David Shearer. When he was five years old my dad went to live with a man named James Coleman. He live with Mr. Coleman for about thirteen years until he left for college. Now I always thought it was odd that a father, David Shearer, would raise all his other children, except for one. That *one* went to live with another man. Rebecca apparently agreed to this arrangement. It makes me wonder if my father's biological father was really James Coleman. Usually about the age of five or so, the resemblance between a child and his father become more apparent. If so, at about five years old, the resemblance between James Coleman and my father may have become more apparent, especially when comparing him to his siblings.

My dad used to mention how his brothers would beat him up when he would try to visit his mother. They would not allow him to see her after he moved in with Mr. Coleman. Before my dad graduated from high school, Mr. Coleman had my dad's last name changed from Shearer to Coleman. So my dad's high school diploma reads "Johnnie Shearer Coleman". Years later, Mr. Coleman died and his daughter came back from her home in Texas for the funeral. She introduced herself to my dad as his sister.

So if my father was the illegitimate child of Rebecca Shearer and James Coleman, he experienced rejection and confusion about his identity at an early age. He had a desire for his mother's love, presence and attention that was never really satisfied. This was in addition to all the racial pressures of deep south Alabama in the

1930's, 40's and 50's. According to him, my dad got beat up trying to go see his mother and beat up by police during the early days of the civil rights movement. No doubt he took an "emotional beating" as well.

I don't know everything that led to John Coleman being who he was, but I think this explains his overall self-centered way of thinking.

As I write this, I see more clearly how the lack of a spiritual foundation, built on the Word of God can lead to "cracks" in our personality, emotions and view of the world. Traumatic events when young can lead to instability in a person's thinking and conduct into adulthood.

In Deuteronomy 6 and 11, the Lord, through Moses, instructs the people to teach His commandments to their children (Deuteronomy 6:7, Deuteronomy 11:19). Children can't fully capture the "meat" of a move of God. They need their parents to provide context, meaning and reminders of events. The most effective learning occurs in "natural", informal settings, e.g., during meal times and times of one-on-one activities. This method of learning helps build a spiritual foundation in children that sets the stage for a deeper personal relationship with God their entire lives. Without it, children are left with their own "natural devices" to deal with the complications of life, which fall woefully short.

You end up with a "cracked" foundation, spiritually, intellectually, and emotionally. You may be able to put up a facade to superficially cover up flaws, but over time and under pressure, the cracks will start to show.

This was my father's foundation; cracked and unable to support what he was supposed to support - his family.

Two contrasting pictures of a "solid" vs. a "cracked" foundation are found in 1 Samuel. In chapter 1, we are told of the birth of the prophet Samuel (the same Samuel who would later anoint David as king). As background read chapters 1 - 3.

In 1 Samuel 1:3 we are told that Samuel's father, Elkanah, went to Shiloh year after year to worship and sacrifice to the Lord. Not only did he lead his family to honor the Lord through worship and sacrifice, but allowed Hannah to dedicate his son to the Lord, his first, and then only son by Hannah. "Dedicate" meant that he turned over his son to the priest of Shiloh (Eli) to be trained and to serve as priest the rest of Samuel's life. This is important because it indicates that there was a God fearing man leading the home.

Hannah, Samuel's mother, provided the other half of the spiritual foundation. In "bitterness of soul" due to being childless and repeatedly taunted by Elkahan's other wife, Hannah prayed to the Lord to have a son (1 Samuel 1:10 - 11). She pledged to give her son back to the Lord "all the days of his life". When she handed over her son to Eli, she even brought items to sacrifice to the Lord (1 Samuel 1:24). She also sung a song to the Lord saying, "My heart rejoices in the Lord…" *after she had given him up.*

So you have two God fearing parents serving as masons, so to speak, in the building of Samuel's spiritual foundation. The Lord used Samuel mightily his entire life, impacting not only kings but an entire nation.

By contrast, God describes Eli's sons as "worthless" or "corrupt". They disrespected the Lord's offering brought by the people and even slept with women who served at the Tent of Meeting. (Note: The "Tent of Meeting" was the place where God would meet with His people before the actual Temple was built by Solomon about 200 years later). In 1 Samuel 2:29, we are told that Eli honored his sons more than the Lord. He did not rebuke nor discipline his sons as he should have, especially since they were serving as priest before a Holy God. As a result, they died relatively young and on the same day. Not only that, the Lord declared that there would not be "...an old man in their family line...", meaning that the men would all die young (1 Samuel 2:30 - 36). So the "cracked" foundation that Eli developed affected not only his sons but his entire family line.

Even though your father may have left you with a "cracked" foundation, God can help you build a solid foundation for your next generation and the ones with whom you have influence.

What kind of foundation will you *choose* to build?

Personal Study

1. Is there anything in the background of your father that would explain or provide a better understanding of his behavior, attitudes, or actions?
2. What kind of foundation was built in his life? What led to him being a "bad" or absent dad?
3. Is your foundation "cracked"? If so, in what way? How have you addressed it?
4. Read Deuteronomy 6:7 and Deuteronomy 11:19. Why does it make sense to follow these commands? Have *you* followed these commands? Why or why not? If not, what are your obstacles? What do you need to change?
5. More importantly, what kind of foundation are you now building in your children and others with whom you have influence? Are you following in your father's footsteps?
6. Read Ephesians 6:4. Explain the verse in your own words. Did your father provoke you? Have you or are you now provoking your children? If so, what effect do you think it will have on their spiritual, intellectual and emotional foundation? What do you need to change?

Notes:

_____

_____

_____

Your Action Plan:

_____

_____

_____

_____

Barriers

One of the issues men deal with concerning "absent" fathers is a barrier to love, or more correctly "honor" their fathers. In Deuteronomy 5, the Israelites had just spent 40 years in the desert and were receiving final instructions from Moses before crossing over to the Promised Land. He instructs them to:

> "Honor your father and your mother, as the Lord your God commanded you, that your days may be long, and that it may go well with you in the land that the Lord your God is giving you." (Deut. 5:16)

He had given the same instructions to their parents 40 years earlier after leaving Egypt (Exodus 21:12). The apostle Paul repeats these instructions in his letter to the Ephesians (Ephesians 6:2 – 3), and even Jesus refers to these instructions when talking to the Rich Young Ruler (Mark 10:17 – 20).

Given so many specific references to "honoring" your father and mother, we can conclude that it must be important to God. But when you talk to men and hear their stories, many, if not most, generally communicate the same message below:

> "My dad wasn't there for me. He didn't care. Obviously I wasn't worth his time. I really don't care if I see him - ever!"

Over time, emotional barriers build walls keeping us from following the Deuteronomy 5:16 commandment and receiving the associated blessing.

Obstacles To Obedience

Many of us can relate to the diagram above. Depending on what our fathers did (or didn't do), our emotions land us in front of one of the four barriers to God's Word. The more intense the emotion, the bigger the barrier.

As I grew from child to young adult, to husband, to step-father, my emotions traveled from irritation towards bitterness...especially after I was married. When my wife and I got married, she already had two sons. I made a choice to raise them as my own to the best of my ability. Almost immediately I was awakened to the amount of time, money, prayer, and dedication it took to raise children. More times than I can count, I gave the last dollar in my wallet to one of our sons so he could go to some function or take care of one of his needs or desires. Every time I did that, throughout the entire 20+ years I've been married, a thought would circulate in the back of my mind:

> "Vic, you weren't worth it...your dad never did this for you. Look at what you're doing for someone else's kids...and you are your dad's own flesh and blood."

Each time the thought would "circulate" in my mind, it left a little residue of negative emotions inside of me. The more it circulated, the more residue was left behind. Unfortunately, we cannot keep negative emotions internal. Eventually they express themselves in some way adversely affecting some other aspect of our lives: our decisions, our health, other relationships.

Meanwhile, my relationship with the Lord had grown to where I knew there was no good outcome to my feelings, so I did what so many of us do — avoided the issue. I took the approach of "Out of sight, out of mind". I avoided seeing or talking to my dad for a number of years. Even when I moved from Texas back to Missouri and lived in the same town, I avoided seeing him.

There was a time when my mom "pushed" to rekindle the relationship between my father and me. She pushed for me to initiate contact, for me to go see him, for me to put forth all the effort to rebuild and maintain the relationship. My dad never reached out to me. I always called him or went to visit him. After engaging in a one-sided relationship for a while, I finally gave up and said:

> "Forget it. If he wants to see me, he can call. At least he can make some effort."

What I resented most about my mother's "push" was that it was one-sided, and pushed me towards some feelings I didn't want to feel:

- Resentment
- Abandonment
- A feeling of not being wanted or good enough
- Anger

There was nothing malicious on my mother's end. She had good intentions - to see the relationship between a son and father restored. But it was her methods with which I disagreed - the persistent push that seemed to occur every other day. Frankly, it was getting on my nerves.

Finally, one day I asked my mom why she pushed so much. Her reply was, "Well, I just want to see you all have a relationship."

With irritation I replied, "Well why don't you push *him?!*"

There was silence. We both knew the answer; my dad wasn't going to allow himself to be pushed into anything, by anyone. Even if it was for *his* good, he would resist being pushed…and would verbally *impress* upon you his desire not to be pushed…in colorful language…if you know what I mean.

What I was looking for was a sign from him that *I* mattered; that *I* was important to him. I was looking for validation from my father…and it never came. Soon after that conversation my mom stopped pushing. I soon gave up the relationship.

A couple of years later I was talking to my uncle, my mother's brother. During the conversation he "strongly" suggested that I restart the relationship with my father. I was surprised that he even mentioned it. He knew that my father had not been a "stellar" husband to his sister. On the surface I wasn't interested. But deep down inside I felt the Lord telling me, "Do what's right."; a repeat of the command of Exodus 21:12.

During the two "silent" years I grew in my relationship with the Lord. My identity and desire to be obedient to Him had grown independent of my relationship with my father. After talking to my uncle, it seems as though the Lord was saying, "Its time. Be obedient to Me, in spite of the barriers."

As a result, I made the *decision* to be obedient. I made the *decision* to honor my dad and respect him as my father, even though I did not get what I considered to be a reciprocal effort. I initiated the calls. I made the visits. I checked on him as a result of a *decision* to be obedient. I did not have expectations of my father. In the past I had gotten no effort from him and I expected nothing in return. The thought that now circulated my mind was:

> "Just be obedient to the Lord."

Little did I know that ten years later that *resolve to be obedient* would be tested to a greater extent than I could imagine.

I share all this to make the following points:

1. Absent fathers can build up negative emotions that produce barriers that keep us from a close personal relationship with the Lord
2. Accumulated negative emotions will most likely affect other relationships in our lives in a negative way
3. The thoughts you "circulate" in your mind will leave a residue, for good or for bad, depending on the thought
4. A maturing (growing) relationship with Christ is the first step in overcoming the negative emotions left by an absent father
5. Honoring your father starts with a *decision* to honor the commandment of God
6. Your relationship with your father may or may not develop to what a father/son relationship should be; the most important thing is that you obey God

There is no substitute for obedience. Read Hebrews 5:7 - 9. Jesus learned obedience through what he suffered. And after He had completed the entire process He became the source of eternal salvation. Obedience is tough sometimes. It often requires a conscience decision on our part, in spite of our feelings. But the benefits can be great. He is our ultimate example.

Is the Lord prompting you to complete some process through obedience, i.e., to be made "perfect"? A process that is unpleasant? A process that may require you to drive across town or pick up a phone? Or a process that requires you to sit down with a mature godly man to help you process your feelings towards a father who my no longer be alive?

Read Isaiah 55:8 - 9. What benefit will you receive after your obedience? More than likely you don't have a clue. God's plan for you is greater than you can imagine. You may pick up the phone to call your father, and impact the life of someone else in a way that is not obvious to you now. God's ways are above our ways. But God always rewards obedience. Read Deuteronomy 28:1 - 14.

Read Psalm 51:10 - 12. The barriers presented in this chapter keep you from God...they pollute your heart. After David's sin with Bathsheba was revealed, he prayed these words to the Lord. Don't let the sin of irritation, anger, bitterness and hatred stand between you and the One who loves you the most. Ask the Lord to create in you a clean heart, and renew a right spirit in you. Keep the barriers between you and the Lord down to a minimum (zero). Nothing that anyone has done to you is worth a barrier between you and your Heavenly Father.

Personal Study

A good guiding principle is given in Hebrews 12:14 – 15. The Amplified Version of the Bible states:

> 14 *Continually* pursue peace with everyone, and the sanctification without which no one will [ever] see the Lord.
>
> 15 See to it that no one falls short of God's grace; that no root of resentment springs up and causes trouble, and by it many be defiled;

1. What are the barriers to your pursuing peace with everyone, including your absent father, if he's still alive? How often does the Lords say we are to pursue peace? What keeps you from being obedient?
2. Is there a "root of resentment" inside you that has caused or is causing trouble for you and others? If so, what do you plan to do about it? Do you need help changing?

Another good Scripture comes from Romans 12: 14 – 21. Read it.

3. Why is this passage so hard to follow in your life? What are your biggest obstacles?
4. If God commands it, then this passage must be possible to achieve or at least to approach. How can it be done? On your strength or His? Elaborate.

Note: We are not going to be held accountable for how someone else responds to us — just our obedience to His Word.

Notes:

_____

_____

_____

Your Action Plan:

_____

_____

_____

_____

Unforgiveness

One day I heard a story of an NFL football player who played with a higher level of intensity than most other players. He almost played "angry" and was widely regarded as a formidable opponent. When asked by a reporter why he played with such intensity, he replied that he thought of his father. He went on to explain that his father abandoned his family when he was young. His mother struggled to support him and his brother throughout his young life. He had vowed that if he ever saw his father again, he would punch him in the face. Thinking of his father is what put him in an "angry" frame of mind.

Playing with intensity is a good thing in professional sports. But the foundation of this player's intensity *on the field* was a deep seated anger towards his absent father *off the field*. Unfortunately this feeling is common among those who feel abandoned. No matter what form the absence takes (physical or emotional), there is still a lasting effect on the children.

Forgiveness Zones

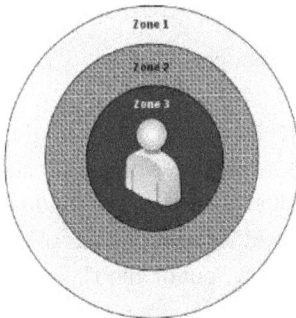

The closer the offense is to you personally, the harder it is to forgive.

The one thing I've noticed in all relationships is that the closer a person is to you, the deeper the wound, and the harder it is to forgive when an offense occurs. To the left is a diagram that illustrates what I mean.

With most people we have a casual relationship. People at work, church, school and our neighborhood are in Zone 1. Generally the words and actions of these people don't bother us much. Emotionally people are kept at a distance. Interactions are usually kept cordial and inconsequential.

As our relationship with people grows, people enter Zone 2. If something is said or done that offends or disappoints us, its effects are long lasting and the "hurt" is at a deeper level.

Offenses from people who reside in Zone 3 (parents, spouses, children, close relatives, intimate friends), have the deepest and most damaging impact on us when an offense occurs. It is at this stage where negative emotions can begin to rule our lives.

With me, I chose to "push" my dad back out to Zone 2 and eventually Zone 1. I chose not to talk or see him for a number of years. Keeping him at a distance meant:

- I would not have to deal with the negative emotions I felt by his apparent lack of love for me.
- I would not feel like I was inconsequential.
- I would not have to think about getting validation from him.
- I would not have to deal with his "guilt trips" he used to throw my way.

In short: out of sight — out of mind…so I thought.

The problem was that I suppressed the feelings; I did not eliminate them. As a result, thoughts and feelings would occasionally circulate in my mind and leave an emotional residue. Overtime, the residue accumulated and began to take its toll on other relationships of my life. So "out of sight" proved not to be totally "out of mind".

In essence, unforgiveness is like a cancer. It starts out small, but over time, if left unchecked, metastasizes into something that is much more harmful.

Cancer and Unforgiveness Stages

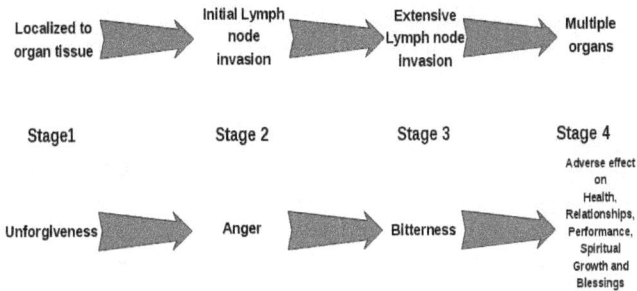

Localized to organ tissue	→	Initial Lymph node invasion	→	Extensive Lymph node invasion	→	Multiple organs
Stage1		Stage 2		Stage 3		Stage 4

				Adverse effect on Health, Relationships, Performance, Spiritual Growth and Blessings
Unforgiveness	→ Anger	→ Bitterness	→	

Note: Stage 0 (in situ) Cancer is in a position where it started. Poses no/little threat to life.

That is one of the reasons the Bible commands us to forgive. In Matthew 6:14 – 15, Jesus instructs us to forgive others. He even warns us of the consequences for not forgiving others – God will not forgive us of our sins.

Again in Mark 11:25, as He instructs His disciples, Jesus tells them to "...forgive, if they have anything against anyone..." (Notice that Jesus did not put conditions on the forgiveness; He said "...*anything* against *anyone*...").

We like to put conditions on forgiveness. In our minds, emotions and hearts we say something like the following:

- I'll forgive once they say they are sorry.
- I'll forgive once they prove to my satisfaction they have met this list of demands I have.
- I'll forgive once they have suffered like I have suffered.
- I'll forgive once I make them pay for what they did to me.
- I'm sorry, I won't forgive.

None of these attitudes are Biblically based. We should be grateful that the Lord doesn't impose one of the conditions on us.

By contrast in Acts 7:59 - 60, Stephen, while being stoned to death cried out to Jesus and said, "Lord, do not hold this sin against them." After that, he died. Stephen was wrongfully accused (Acts 6:8 - 13); he knew that, but yet made a decision to ask for forgiveness for his executioners.

Jesus provided the ideal example of forgiveness. On the cross, close to death, Jesus appeals to God to forgive those who crucified Him. (Luke 23:33 – 35).

Now you may say:

> "Well that's fine for Jesus..He was God. But I ain't Jesus and I hurt!"

How are we to forgive when we hurt so bad? When the pain has moved to Stage 3?

First, we need to understand that *to forgive* means: "*to release, to send away, to permit to depart*". It is a **choice**, not a **feeling**. It is saying:

> "I release you from the debt you owe me. I also release my 'right' to pay you back for the wrong you've done me."

Forgiveness does not address the legitimacy of the offense. Anger at the offense may be "justified", but forgiveness focuses on the one who has been offended **choosing** to release the offender. The first step in the forgiveness *process* is an awareness that God has forgiven us and has reconciled us to Himself. The cost of that reconciliation was the shed blood of His Son. The second step of the process is making a **decision** to forgive. Feelings change later in the process.

My immediate benefit to deciding to forgive my father was being able to live at peace inside. *Forgiveness brings peace to the mind and emotions.* My second benefit was that I'm assured that God would forgive me of my offenses towards Him (Matthew 6:14 – 15). My third benefit was being able to be a witness to my sons. They knew that my father and I were not close and he was not a part of my life growing up. So they have had an opportunity to see forgiveness in action.

(Note: I've never provided any of the "dirty details" of the relationship to my sons. My detailing his actions/inactions would require me to relive the events. I did not want to put myself in a position where I would soon find myself communication more *emotion* than *events*. Their witness of forgiveness could be easily clouded by my emotions. Details were not necessary).

Was it difficult to do? Yes. Did it take time for the emotions to subside? Yes. Did it take time for the whole process to occur? Yes. Was it a series of choices to "release" during the process? Yes. Would I do it again? Yes. Why? The biggest reason is that it puts me in right relationship with my Heavenly Father. When it's all said and done, my personal relationship with God the Father, through Christ, by the power of the indwelling Holy Spirit, is at stake. I value that relationship too much to allow a "cancer" to spread.

So what will *you* choose? Peace and unity with God or "cancer"? We all know the end result of cancer if left untreated.

Personal Study

1. In general, why is forgiveness so important?
2. Why is forgiveness to hard?
3. What are the top two obstacles that keep you from forgiving your father?
4. What "after effects" have you seen or experienced from your unforgiveness of others?
5. What "after effects" have you experienced by not being forgiven by others?

Read Ephesians 1:7 and Ephesians 4:32.

5. Why is receiving God's forgiveness so important?
6. What would life be like for you if God took on your attitude towards forgiveness?

Read Romans 3:23.

7. Explain the verse in your own words.
8. How does this apply to your father? How does this apply to you?

Notes:
_____
_____
_____

Your Action Plan:
_____
_____
_____
_____

Legacy

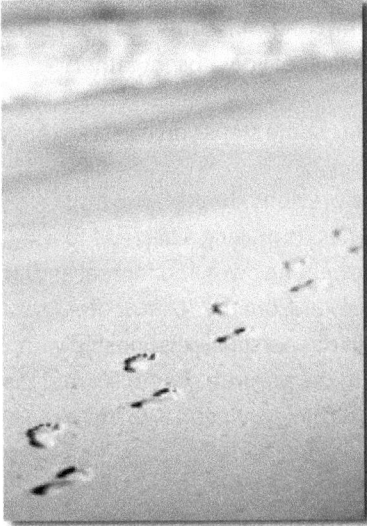

Legacy: *anything handed down from the past, as from an ancestor or predecessor*

Everybody will have one...good or bad...high impact or barely noticed, but everyone who walks the earth will have a legacy. We interact with people, we form relationships, we father and raise children, we go to school and work and church...all of these activities have impacts on other people. Some effects last only for a short time. Other effects last not only for our life time, but for generations.

What will be your legacy? What do you desire it to be? What have you established so far?

These are important questions. They provide the foundation for the purpose of your life, your existence. Even an absent father has a legacy. Most often his effect on the family is negative due to his absence. Statistics show children from single parent homes are more likely to:

- Have emotional and behavioral problems
- Perform poorly in school
- Have higher high school dropout rates
- Have more encounters with law enforcement
- Have more substance abuse problems
- And most importantly...extend this legacy of "absent fathers" to the next generation.

As you think about how you've responded to your absent father, what legacy are you building? Is it the one you'd like to be remembered for? Are you following in the footsteps you swore you would never follow? Are you encountering consequences from the buildup of negative emotions as a result of your absent father?

Do you want to change? Let's outline some steps you can take today:

Forgive your father: As stated in the previous chapter, you must forgive your absent father. Forgiveness is making a *decision* to release your absent father from the debt he owes you for real and/or *perceived* offenses. Forgiveness frees us from the "cancer of bitterness" which will be a barrier in our personal relationship with the Lord. When you are dealing with the purpose of your life and the effect on future generations, the last thing you need is to be disconnected from your Creator.

Grow in your personal relationship with the Lord: In the letter to the Ephesians, the apostle Paul prayed that God would give the Ephesian Christians "…the Spirit of wisdom and of revelation in the knowledge of Him…" (Ephesians 1:16 – 21). Why? The same power that raised Christ from the dead would be available and active in them to accomplish the purposes of God for their lives. A legacy that glorified God would be made possible.

Understand that a powerful Biblical legacy is tied to the Word of God: Proverbs 19:21 teaches us that we may have many intentions and plans in our hearts, (some may be good, and some may be bad), but it is God's counsel that prevails. And what is His counsel? The principles, commands, and laws established in His Word. God's plan for your life is always best; He wants you to make wise decisions your entire life (see the previous verse, Proverbs 19:20). Living a life of wisdom based on the Word of God will lead to a powerful legacy. We just have to submit to Him.

Read James 4:6 - 8. Now the word "submit" has a connotation in our society of being weak and conquered. But the word "submit" is translated from the word "hupotassó" which literally means "to arrange under". So when we "submit" ourselves to God, we are saying that we will make choices to arrange ourselves under His leadership, principles, commands, and laws; namely His Word. Doing so, will put ourselves in position to receive His best, not only for us but for our children and others we influence, i.e., our legacy.

Now you may say, "Vic that's fine, but my dad didn't leave me with a thing, no love, no acceptance, and certainly no money. I'm still 'ticked off' about it. I feel I was abandoned."

Psalm 27:9 – 11 says:

> *Hide not your face from me. Turn not your servant away in anger, O you who have been my help. Cast me not off; forsake me not, O God of my salvation! For my father and my mother have forsaken me, but the Lord will take me in. Teach me your way, O Lord, and lead me on a level path because of my enemies.*

Is this the cry of your heart? Sometimes are you in so much pain due to your abandonment, that you feel like David? He speaks directly to your situation…*God will take you in if your mother and father forsakes you*. You are never abandoned by Him.

Speaking to this point, I came to a point in my life where I had to change my mindset and think of God as being my "real" father. To become better as a man, father and husband, I had to associate with godly men who supported me in my struggles. In considering God as my "real" dad, I had to talk to him on a regular basis, share my concerns and seek His guidance. In short, I had to make God *real* to deal with *real* problems…and He showed Himself to be *real*. He will do the same for you.

Understand that God is sovereign and His ways are far above your ways; He is in charge of the "big picture": One of my favorite Scripture passages is Isaiah 55:8 – 13. It comes up so often in my life, it's like God is telling me:

"Look Vic, I not only see the big picture, I created the big picture for your life before you were born. You won't be able to understand all the details of your life because my Word works in so many ways…some obvious, some subtle, some quickly, some delayed. Just trust Me and watch and see the results."

If you forgive your father and others who have offended you, grow in your personal relationship with God, submit to God's plan for your life, you will see the type of legacy that ultimately glorifies Him. The results will be good. Isaiah 55:13 speaks of good things resulting from the working of His Word.

Remember that "More is caught than taught": This happens to be a quote from my pastor Bryant Lee. Kids learn more from observing our behavior than what we tell them. If they see us consistently acting in a foolish manner, they will tend to mimic that behavior. If they see us consistently acting in a godly manner, they will tend to mimic that behavior. How we behave establishes what's "normal" to our children (and the young folks around us)…craziness or godliness. Our behavior begins to shape the legacy we will leave.

How do you implement this plan? It all falls back to a *decision* to change and build your personal relationship with God. If you need help (and we all do at times), find a couple of mature godly men to walk with you in your journey. Be open to godly, Biblical correction.

The steps above mainly deal with a "renewing of your mind", i.e., how you think, your mindset. How you think will determine how you act. If you set your mind and heart to leave a godly legacy, in spite of what was left for you, God is there to help you.

Our time, talents, beliefs and decisions are like paints on a pallet that can be used to create the picture of our legacy.

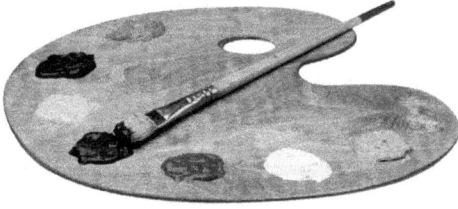

So what's it gonna be? Will you chose to paint this:

Or this:

The decision is yours.

Personal Study

What do you want your legacy to be in your family?

_____

What do you want your legacy to be in your occupation?

_____

What do you want your legacy to be in your social circle?

_____

What do you want your legacy to be as it pertains to your spiritual life?

_____

Read Colossians 1:9 - 14.
1. Why is that a good prayer to pray over your family and your circle of influence?
2. How will it relate to your legacy?

Notes:

_____
_____
_____

Your Action Plan:

_____
_____
_____
_____

A Time of Separation

The relationship between my father and me has been complicated to say the least. When I was young, I was actually afraid of my father. He used to come home from work (or a night at the bar) and was very intimidating and demanding. He used to put my mom and me on the defensive by his aggressive behavior. After a while, being on the defensive became normal. Arguments between my parents were common, especially late at night. Many times I would hear ash trays thrown around and after a good hour or so of cussing, he would slam the door leaving the house. He wouldn't come home until early the next morning.

My parents divorced when I was 13 years old. I saw my mom working double shifts to earn extra money. My father had run up the credit card balances and left my mom to pay them off. He was supposed to pay $200/month child support, which was a huge amount back in the early 70's, but needless to say, we never saw a dime.

After the divorce, my father's visits became non-existent as well as his phone calls. The times I did reach out to call him, I was usually put on the defensive - the norm. Comments like, "Well, it's about time you called me..." or "Well, it sure took you long enough to call..." were common. "Guilt trips" finally took their toll when I was in college.

My first year in college, I excelled academically. It was almost like an extension of high school, where I could get whatever grade I wanted just by putting forth the effort. *I* was in control. There were no limits to what *I* could do. And then (…can you guess…), the bottom fell out the second semester of my sophomore year.

At the same time, the relationship with my dad started to take a toll on me. Internally, I felt like I needed to stay in touch with my father and keep the relationship going, but I "paid a price" every time we talked. I took on the responsibility of managing our relationship, unaware of the father's responsibility in a father-son relationship. Emotionally I became "frazzled". At the same time, my college classes became more difficult. I majored in chemical engineering which was one of the harder engineering fields. The result – my grades started to drop. According to my freshman year expectations, a "B" was acceptable as long as it was associated with at least three A's to cover it. Well, over time my expectations were adjusted to where a "C" was a welcomed sight.

I was in a battle. Attacks were coming from:

1. The responsibility of maintaining the relationship between me and my father
2. Dealing with guilt trips every time he and I would talk
3. Increasing frustration of dropping grades
4. Increasing frustration of not being able to control my situation
5. Most importantly, being ignorant of my need to acknowledge God in my life

I truly didn't know the Lord personally at that time and was focused on *my* will, *my* ability, and *my* control to get what *I* wanted. It was all about me *without* God.

Three things happened during this time that changed my life:

I began to seek the Lord…to really seek Him as heartfelt as I could at the time. This was the first time I encountered a situation that I could not control. I was humbled and brought to a realization that in life I was *not* in total control. I started to learn that I may have influence over a situation, but never *total* control. That belongs to God and Him alone.

The lesson I started to learn: *God is sovereign. We are not.* The reason I say "started to learn" is because I had a tendency to slip back to my old ways.

Secondly, I readjusted my focus from the grade (like getting an "A") to doing my best. My Fluid Dynamics instructor was Dr. X. B. Reed. After taking his tests, I used to think that X. B. stood for "X-tra Brutal". This was one of the courses where earning a "C" was a victory.

After getting "brutalized" on one of his tests, I went to see him in his office. I asked him what I could do to perform better on his tests. I was studying as best I could. I just couldn't seem to do well. And he told me something that has stuck with me over the years.

He said, "Well Mr. Coleman did you do your best?"

I replied, "Yes".

"Then you've done all you can do at this time. You can't do better than your best, can you?"

"Well, no, I guess not." I replied thoughtfully.

"Continue to do your best and focus on that".

The conversation was over. And no, he did not slack up on his tests; they continued to be "X-tra Brutal".

I had put extra pressure on myself trying to achieve an "A" (amidst all the emotional things going on with my father). My lack of success just led to more frustration. Initially when I took one of his tests, I was more focused on *the consequences of not performing well, rather than the material in front of me.* There were many times when I would study with some friends and help them prepare, and come out of the test with a lower grade than they had achieved. This just increased my anxiety on the next test.

But after talking to Dr. Reed, it was like a weight lifted off of me. Mentally and emotionally I started to shift my focus to doing my best, and letting the results come as they may. I would learn from my mistakes and focus on improving the next time. As a result the anxiety level during tests dropped significantly and my grades started to improve.

The third and more relevant thing that changed in me is that I stopped talking to my father. The emotional drain was so severe that I had to "cut him off" so to speak. Naturally he did not try to call me at all. We ended up not talking for seven years…afterwards I initiated the call. There was a time of separation.

With the separation, came stability in my emotions. I was able to think and function like "normal" folks. For several years I kept some level of emotional separation from him…more like a protective screen.

Now for applicable Scriptures.

The first one that comes to mind is Colossians 3:21.

> Fathers, do not provoke your children, lest they become discouraged. (ESV)

The word "provoke" has a sense of being provoked, irritated, or aroused for a prolonged period of time. Being "provoked" for a long period of time can have some significant adverse effects on children.

Ephesians 6:4 has a similar message. Another is Psalm 27:9 – 10.

> Hide not your face from me. Turn not your servant away in anger, O you who have been my help. Cast me not off; forsake me not, O God of my salvation!

*For my father and my mother have forsaken me, but
the Lord will take me in.* (ESV)

This is the cry of a person's heart who feels rejected. He cries out to
the Lord, Who will take him in.

For years I struggled with suppressed feelings of rejection. Thoughts
would go through my mind like:

> "If you weren't valuable enough for your father to
> support you, what good are you?"

Crazy thinking, but real feelings.

Emotions became more "potent" after I married and started raising
children who weren't my own. When I got married I made a
commitment to raise my wife's sons as if they were my own, to the
best of my ability. Over the years I saw how much time, attention,
prayer, sacrifice, money, and dedication it took to raise kids. After
addressing a need of one of our sons, occasionally I would entertain
thoughts like:

> "Wow…I wasn't worth this type of effort."

I began to combat the thoughts and their destructive emotions by
meditating on the Word. Meditating on Psalm 27:9 – 10 and Psalms
34:18 brought me closer to the Lord. This led me to think of God as
my "real" Father. Our relationship grew as a result. The closer I drew
to Him, the more peace I received. As a result, I was able to better
lead my family in a godly way.

None of us have perfect parents, but we do have a perfect God who
desires to have a heartfelt, growing personal relationship with Him.
My time of separation from my earthly father was used to become
more acquainted with my Heavenly Father.

I share all this because:

- I know other men struggle inwardly with absent, imperfect fathers. There is hope in Christ.
- We all will leave a legacy, intentional or not. I want to encourage men not to pass on damage (residue) to the next generation. *Hurting people hurt people.* Christ came to give us life; an abundant life that is the foundation of a godly, rich and powerful legacy. (John 10:10)

If you are separated from your earthly father, use this time as an opportunity to become personally acquainted with your Heavenly Father, through a relationship with Christ, being empowered by the Holy Spirit to be the man God has intended you to be. And do not isolate yourself, but begin to associate with wise, mature, godly men who can help you in your daily struggles. That's what brothers in Christ are all about.

Personal Study

Read Romans 12:1 - 2.
1. As it pertains to your father, what kind of thoughts generally come to mind? Are they positive or negative?
2. What feelings come with those thoughts?

Read Ephesians 4:20 - 24.
3. What do you "feed your mind" on a daily basis, i.e., what do you watch, listen to, and read?
4. The passage refers to being "...made new in the attitude of your minds...". What is the best way to renew the attitude of your mind in a positive way?

Read Philippians 4:8 - 9.
5. What actions do you need to take to fulfill this command?
6. What do you think the results will be when you do?

Notes:
_____
_____
_____

Your Action Plan:
_____
_____
_____

Buried, But Alive

One of the things I love about Jesus is that He used very common concepts to illustrate and reveal very deep principles of the Gospel. One of the concepts He used in His parables was the concept of seeds.

In Matthew 13 Jesus teaches people about the Kingdom of God through three parables involving seeds: *Parable of the Sower*, *Parable of the Weeds*, and the *Mustard Seed and Leaven* (yeast).

The people of that time lived in an agrarian society, so farming was a way of life. Everyone understood the idea of planting a seed in the ground and over time producing a crop. The crop you received depended on the type of seed you planted. Other factors involved are the soil, water, and sun. What's amazing is the fact that on the surface, a seed looks dead, inanimate. But unlike rocks, under the right conditions, a seed will come alive and bare crops.

When we are dealing with an absent father, whether he is absent physically, emotionally or spiritually, many types of seeds are planted inside of us. Some common ones are:

- Anger/bitterness
- A lack of self worth
- A "driving" desire to be approved or accepted by others
- A false perception of God

- No sense of God, at all
- A lack of discipline
- A lack of trust
- Selfishness
- Insecurity

There are many others. The problem is that these "seeds" are not dead; they are buried, but alive. Under the right conditions they will produce crops, over time, at different stages of our lives. The consequences of these crops are evident throughout our society:

- Overflowing prisons and jails
- Epidemic substance abuse problems
- Ignorance of and misconceptions of manhood
- Broken families and relationships
- A denial and/or disrespect for God and godly things

And the list goes on.

God, in His grace, has given us guidelines, principles and commands to combat the growth of "ugly crops" in our lives. I present some of these to communicate what worked in my life, and people I've known over the years. These principles work. Why? They come from the Manufacturer, the One who created us and knows everything about us.

First of all, we need to address the most common and destructive seed: anger which stems from unforgiveness. As I stated in an earlier chapter, anger that stems from unforgiveness is like a cancer. If you address it early, then most of its toxic effects can be avoided. But if left "untreated", unforgiveness will produce crops which will destroy not only your life, but the lives of others. Jesus says in Matthew 6:14 – 15, that if we forgive others, then God will forgive us. With respect to our absent fathers, the result could possibly lead to restored relationships. But most importantly, it will result in a restored, stronger relationship with God.

To implement forgiveness, we have to "choose" to say:

> "You do not have to repay me for the wrong you've done me, perceived or real."

Make a *choice* to release them from the debt they owe you. Negative feelings will eventually subside. We are not to live based on our feelings. The process of forgiveness goes something like this:

- Choice first ⇒ feelings later
- Internal change first ⇒ external changes later
- Internal peace first ⇒ external peace later

The seed of anger also leads to another crop: hot temper. People like this are unpleasant to be around and generally cause trouble, not only in their own lives but in the lives of others as well. Proverbs 15:18 says:

> *A hot-tempered man stirs up strife, but he who is slow to anger quiets contention. (ESV)*

The Bible instructs us to strive for restoration and to live in peace with others. Then the God of love and peace will be with us. (2 Corinthians 13:11). Philippians 4:6 – 9 states:

> *…do not be anxious about anything, but in everything by prayer and supplication with thanksgiving let your requests be made known to God. And the peace of God, which surpasses all understanding, will guard your hearts and your minds in Christ Jesus.*
>
> *Finally, brothers, whatever is true, whatever is honorable, whatever is just, whatever is pure, whatever is lovely, whatever is commendable, if there is any excellence, if there is anything worthy of praise, think about these things. What you have learned and received and heard and seen in*

*me—practice these things, and the God of peace will
be with you. (ESV)*

Again, it starts with a choice...a choice to pray to God, with
thanksgiving. Now you may be thinking:

> "Lord, I'm actually mad at you. You could have
> made that man do right and save me and my family
> some grief. But You didn't. So how can I be
> thankful to You. I ain't feelin' it."

If this is you, that's okay. God has heard it before. What He's after is
a relationship with you that is so deep, that others will want to know
what you know about Him. As you choose to draw closer to Him in
spite of your feelings, the very nature of that unity (peace) will
change you internally so you can be a help to others. In the end God
will receive the glory. That's really what 2 Corinthians 1:3 - 11 is all
about. God comforts us so we can be a comfort to others.

So to keep the "ugly seeds" from producing "ugly crops" in your
lives, you have to change the environment in which the seeds grow -
your mind and your heart (the real you). That can only be done
through unity (peace) with God. That can only occur through:

- Faith in Him and His Son
- Prayer, which involves *two-way* communication (not just
  you talking, but also listening)
- Reading and meditating on His Word

This process will transform us into the image of Christ...a likeness of
Him.

Be wise and understand that seeds of an absent father are not dead
and buried, but alive. If left unattended, they will produce crops of
destruction in your life. Also be wise and realize that the only true
way to change the soil permanently is to "saturate the soil" in the

Word of God, which is the foundation for unity (peace) with God. The solution is straight forward.

So, will you choose to change the soil? Remember, seeds, both good and bad, are buried and alive.

Personal Study

One of my favorite passages (or maybe the one He's trying to get me to truly understand) is Isaiah 55:8 – 13. In it God talks about His Word accomplishing the purpose for which He sent it.

Read Isaiah 55:8 - 13.

1. What does "rain" and "snow" do for crops? What does the Word of God do for us?
2. Does rain or snow immediately produce "bread for the eater"? If not, what has to happen? What is the process?
3. What process can we expect the Word of God to implement in our lives?

Read Isaiah 55:6 - 7.

4. What can we expect if we turn away from wicked ways and thoughts? If we don't, what can we expect?
5. What seeds are "cultivating" inside of you? What crops have you produced? What seeds are you planting in the lives your family?

Notes:

_____
_____
_____

Your Action Plan:

_____
_____
_____

The Final Chapter

As I stated earlier, for several years my father and I lived in the same town but did not speak to each other. He didn't call me and I didn't call him. One day, at the insistence of my uncle, I started to call and visit my father. What was unusual about the situation was that my uncle was my *mother's* brother, not one of my father's brothers. His brothers had all died by then. My uncle was fully aware of my father's history and ways. He knew that my father had not been a "model husband" to his sister, but yet he insisted that I see him — strongly and persistently.

I was compelled to follow through and see my dad. Due in part to my uncle's insistence, but also to an "urging" inside, namely it was the "Christian thing to do" (Deuteronomy 5:16, Ephesians 6:3).

So, I started to visit my dad. We developed a relationship, somewhat awkward, but more than what we had. I intentionally avoided bringing up things from the past. I was focused on rebuilding, not tearing down. I would give periodic reports to my uncle when he asked how things were going.

In the Sermon on the Mount, Jesus provided the multitudes who came to see Him a model prayer. We commonly call it "The Lord's Prayer" (Matthew 6:9 – 13). In the passage at the end of the model prayer, the Lord spends verses 12, 14 and 15 on one topic — forgiveness. So it must be important to Him. And what's important to Him, needs to be important to me.

I had to begin the process of forgiving my dad. To be honest, at first, I didn't "feel it". The "movie" playing in my mind was a replay of past events, and with it, all the associated emotions of anger, rejection, etc. The more the "movie" played, the more intense the emotions became. Anger, if left to cultivate, grows into bitterness. So I had to "change the channel" so to speak; think about something else. The scriptures give clear instructions regarding our thoughts (Philippians 4:8, Isaiah 55:7). Another good one is Isaiah 59:7, but read it in context with the entire passage, Isaiah 59:1 – 8. Make sure your unforgiveness doesn't put you in the category of verse 2.

Over about a two year period I noticed several things about him. He was becoming more paranoid and forgetful. He was convinced that someone was listening to our conversation when we talked on the phone. He was so articulate and convincing, it was hard to tell if he was imagining things or telling the truth. Also, his house became more and more messy; almost in disarray. Things got so bad that my mom sent her housekeeper over to clean my dad's house. Everytime the housekeeper went, the cleaning became a bigger job. Pots in the kitchen looked like he had burned the food while cooking in them.

Then one day I received a job offer and moved from Missouri to Texas. I left both parents in Missouri. Whenever I came back to visit my mom, I would make time to visit my dad.

In the spring of 2015, my mom succumbed to cancer. I talked to my dad and offered to pick him up for the funeral and burial. But he said he would drive himself and would be there for both. Well…he didn't show up. Nor did he call. Now this was the perfect opportunity for me to "cut him off for life". I was hurt. He promised me he would be there and he wasn't. My mom was one of the two or three people who truly cared about him, even though they had been divorced for over 40 years. My mom used to say that he lived like a hermit; he shunned everyone. (Amazingly enough, neither one had remarried.)

In my mind there was no excuse to miss my mom's funeral. Being an only child, I had to make all the funeral arrangements, see my mom's body before the viewing, speak at her funeral and see her buried. He didn't have to participate in the preparation of any of that; I took care of all the details. All he had to do was show up like he said he would. He didn't and he didn't call. I felt he disrespected me and especially my mom.

As I said, it was the perfect opportunity to "cut him off"…but I didn't. I *chose* not to. I made a decision in spite of my emotions. This was another step in the process of forgiveness…even when I felt that unforgiveness was "justifiable".

As an aside, there is an acronym that I heard from Charles Stanley (senior pastor at First Baptist of Atlanta), years ago that applies here. It is H.A.L.T. He said in effect, don't make major decisions when you are Hungry, Angry, Lonely or Tired. Under those conditions, you are less likely to make decisions based on the will of God, and more likely to make decisions based on your current emotional state. This was one of those occasions. My decision to *not* cut my dad off was made *after* the funeral, *after* I returned to Texas, and *after* the anger subsided. I called him about a month *after* the burial.

When I called my dad, I never talked about the funeral or asked him his reasons for not coming; he never volunteered an explanation either. I kept the conversation in "safe mode" in an attempt to maintain our relationship.

(In the Microsoft Windows® operating system, you can boot and start your computer in "safe mode". This is a condition where the computer starts up with a minimal number of programs running. This is done when the computer is prone to slow performance and/or crashes. Safe mode is an attempt to avoid loading the software that causes problems for you. I chose to keep the relationship between me and my father in "safe mode".)

Soon after returning to Texas I helped my father get a cell phone. This allowed us to talk without the conversations being "eavesdropped". (As mentioned earlier, paranoia was a major factor in his thinking). We soon ran into problems with his ability to operate a smartphone. It had no buttons like older phones. It was what he wanted, but proved to be too "modern" for him. He eventually stopped using it and began saying that it was probably bugged too. He also said he had his home phone cut off. Later I discovered that the phone was off because the bill had not been paid.

Then one day I received a call from a social worker at the VA hospital in the city where my dad lived (he was a veteran). She told me that he had gone to the bank to withdraw some money and the teller noticed he was acting oddly. The bank personnel called the State of Missouri. Well long story short, he was diagnosed with moderate Alzheimer's disease. At that time finances were tight for me and my wife. I had been laid off during a downturn in the oil and gas industry the year before, but scraped up enough money to drive up to Missouri to check on him.

His single message to me during my visit to the VA hospital was: "Get me out of here so I can go home!" But there was little I could do at the time. He ended up staying there for several months. The hospital could not release him to live on his own. He needed to have someone watch over him. Eventually the VA and state of Missouri were ready to put him in a nursing home.

My dad's house was in ill repair. It was really in no condition for him to live by himself safely. He was in "ill repair" himself. I looked for a house sitter and/or nurse, but they were too expensive. So the only other option was to bring my dad back to Texas to live with my wife and me. Living in the same house with John Coleman was the last thing I'd thought would ever happen. A year earlier I felt like "cutting him off". Now I was bringing him into my home to care for him. Amazing.

By that time I had found a job, but was undergoing radiation treatments for prostate cancer. So one day in June, I postponed about a week's worth of radiation treatments, drove to Missouri with my wife, packed up my dad and brought him back to Texas. We arrived back home on Father's Day. I looked forward to this being an opportunity to rebuild our "lost" years; to truly get to know him. I knew who my father was (i.e., his identify), but I never really knew the man; he always kept a barrier up so you couldn't get too close to him.

Well my dad lived with us for ten months, and needless to say, it was "eventful". A common experience of families with Alzheimer's relatives is that the ones closest to the ones afflicted are the people who receive the most "grief", i.e., the Alzheimer's patients typically are mean to the people closest to them. This was certainly true in my situation. My wife was okay; my dad liked her. But with me, he was "as mean as a rattlesnake" at times, as they say in Texas.

He was suspicious of me, spoke harshly to me, spoke badly about me to others. He stretched the truth about me so much that it lost its shape, in other words, he lied about me to others, as well as to me directly. It was rough. He was so articulate and practiced in his responses that if you didn't know he had Alzheimer's, you'd think he was in his right mind and what he was saying was true.

(Apparently I must have signed up for an advanced course in forgiveness. I just didn't know it.)

After ten long months, my wife and I were both stressed to the max. The aggression, tension, and physical care he required was more than we could handle. It was actually a tough decision for me, but I had to place my dad in an assisted living facility. It was a tough decision because in a way, I felt I was giving up on him. It was my responsibility to take care of my father, but he needed more care than we could give. It was a necessary decision.

After about two months he was placed in the memory care section of that facility. This was for patients who showed signs of severe Alzheimer's. Some severe Alzheimer's patients have a tendency to wander, so a secured facility is necessary. My dad liked to "walk", if you know what I mean. He also showed tendencies of aggression towards others.

To make a long story short, after about a year, my dad was rushed to the ER. He was diagnosed with a heart condition where his aortic valve opened only 16% of normal...and the condition would get progressively worse over time. (The aortic valve is in the main artery that distributes blood from the heart to the rest of the body). He made a second trip to the ER the following month. After this second trip he was placed on Hospice.

My dad lived ten months while on Hospice. Then finally two days before Christmas he passed away quietly in his sleep. He was 87 years old.

You would think that the complex nature of our relationship would have ended on December 23rd. But it didn't. It just so happened it was the holiday season and there was a US government shutdown underway. I wasn't able to bury my father until January 9th of the next year. It seems like every aspect of our relationship was complex, even getting him buried.

Given our Alzheimer's influenced, contentious relationship, he and I never got a chance to directly talk about his accepting Christ in his life while he was living with us. Every time we started a conversation about the Lord, or what I had been reading in the Bible, he would immediately lose interest and start yawning. Spiritual conversations with me (who writes Bible studies regularly), were conversations that he cut short or avoided all together. It wasn't until he was literally on his deathbed that I was able to talk to him about the Lord and lead him in the prayer of salvation. Now he was unable to talk at that time, but he could hear and respond subtly. Now, do I know for sure he accepted Christ as his Savior...no. I just did my part. He did seem to respond slightly though. Jesus said that if you lift Him up *He* would draw all men towards Him (John 12:32). I did my part and the rest was up to Christ.

Now, I don't have all the answers or full understanding of all the "why's" of my becoming my father's keeper. But what I do know is found in Isaiah 55:8 - 9: my thoughts are not His thoughts, nor are my ways His ways.

So don't be surprised if your life takes a twist involving your father. God can take any difficult situation and make something good come from it. You just have to be willing and say, "Yes Lord", when He calls.

Personal Study

1. When was the last time you made a decision where you broke the H.A.L.T rule? What were the results? Looking back, would you change your decision or done things a different way?

Read Isaiah 30:18 - 23.

2. According to verse 18, what is the desire of God's heart?
3. According to verse 19, what do you have to do?
4. When was the last time you came to the Lord with the issue between you and your father? Were you open to His leading in addressing that issue? If not, why?
5. Verse 22 speaks of idols. Are there idols in your life, i.e., things or thoughts or desires that come before God?
6. If so, why are they there? If so, do you truly intend to repent, i.e., turn around and/or release it? If not, why?
7. According to verse 23, what will God do when you release your idols?

Notes:

_____

_____

_____

Your Action Plan:

_____

_____

_____

Digging Deeper

1. What are your biggest challenges in the relationship and/or residue of your relationship with your father?

2. How do you plan to address/overcome those challenges?

3. Do you have any anger towards God for what your father did or didn't do? If so, why? What do you plan to do about that anger towards the Lord? Is letting it fester an option?

4. Based on the Scriptures presented in this book which ones do you think will help you the most with anger towards God? Which ones will help you the most with anger towards your father?

5. What type of legacy are you leaving with your children, spouse and circle of influence?

6. If the legacy is not what you want, what are your biggest challenges? What are the first two things you need to do to change that legacy?

7. Do you think you could be (or have been) your father's keeper? If not, why? If so, how did it come to pass?

8. Name two godly, mature men who can walk with you in your journey.

_____

_____

9. When do you plan to reach out to these men for help?

_____

10. Name three goals you will achieve in the next 30 days as it pertains to your father, your legacy, your relationship with Christ or other relationships.

_____

_____

_____

11. Name three goals for the next 60 days.

_____

_____

_____

12. Name three goals for the next 90 days.

_____

_____

_____

Share these with the godly men you identified above so that they will hold you accountable.

Personal Journal

Date:

_____

_____

_____

_____

_____

Date:

_____

_____

_____

_____

_____

Date:

_____

_____

_____

_____

_____

Date:

_____

_____

_____

_____

_____

Date:

Date:

Date:

Date:

Date:

Date:

Date:

Date:

Date:

Date:

www.ingramcontent.com/pod-product-compliance
Lightning Source LLC
Chambersburg PA
CBHW060616030426
42337CB00018B/3068